DAILY
mindfulness

COLLECTION OF QUOTES & JOURNALING PROMPTS FOR SELF-DISCOVERY

BY FAE AMARA SAGE

ORIGINAL TITLE:
"Daily Mindfulness: Collection of
Quotes and Journaling Prompts for
Self-Discovery"

ISBN 978-9916-4-1763-8

Welcome to "**Daily Mindfulness: Collection of Quotes and Journaling Prompts for Self-Discovery**".

Within this book you will find a collection of deeply enlightening words of wisdom as well as reflective journaling prompts that are designed to help you gain insight into your inner world and cultivate a deeper sense of self-awareness and acceptance.

Whether you are new to mindfulness or an experienced practitioner, my hope for you is that this book offers you a daily dose of inspiration and insights that will lovingly support you on your journey towards greater presence, calmness, and personal growth.

Happy exploration,

Fae Amara

stay focused on

your dreams

AND WORK DILIGENTLY TO
BRING THEM INTO REALITY

JOURNALING PROMPT 1

Take a deep breath and start paying attention to your headspace. Take 5 minutes to write down your thoughts - just let them flow in a non-judgmental way. Notice the quality of those thoughts - are they slow, calm, rapid, or reoccurring? Do they have an underlying theme?

It was when I stopped searching for home within others, and lifted the fountations of home within myself, I found there were no roots more intimate than those between a mind and body that have decided to be whole.

JOURNALING PROMPT 2

What is something that I am grateful for in my life right now? Why is it important & valuable to me?

"Your calm mind is
the ultimate
weapon against
your challenges. So
relax."

BRYANT MCGILL

JOURNALING PROMPT 3

What are my core values? How do
they influence my decision-making
and behaviors?

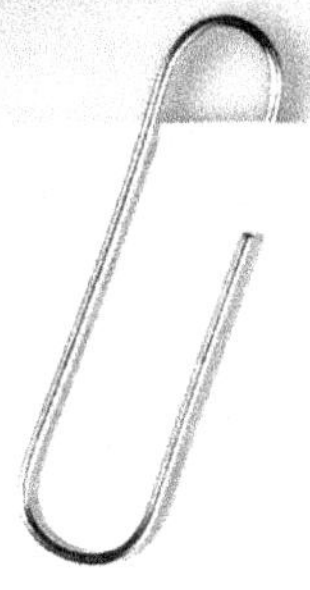"The body benefits from movement, and the mind benefits from stillness."

Sakyong Mipham

JOURNALING PROMPT 4

What is a fear that I have been holding onto? How has it held me back from pursuing my dreams and goals? How can I start to question it, or perhaps even make friends with it?

"The still waters of a lake reflect the beauty around it. When the mind is still, the beauty of the self is reflected."

JOURNALING PROMPT 5

What are some healthy boundaries that I can set in my life and within my relationships with others? How can I communicate my needs effectively?

"You are the sky.
Everything else is
just the weather."

Pema Chodron

JOURNALING PROMPT 6

What are some things that I can do to cultivate more ease and happiness in my life?

How can I prioritize joy and playfulness?

How do you make time for myself each day?

YOU ARE NOT THE VOICE OF YOUR MIND.

Be the silent watcher of your thoughts and behaviour. You are beneath the thinker. You are the stillness beneath the mental noise. You are the love and joy beneath the pain."

ECKHART TOLLE

JOURNALING PROMPT 7

Write down 5 affirmations that you can use to cultivate more self-love and acceptance. How can you practice these affirmations daily?

"How we pay attention to the present moment largely determines the character of our experience, and therefore, the quality of our lives."

– Sam Harris

JOURNALING PROMPT 8

What are some of my biggest strengths and accomplishments? How can I use them to overcome challenges in my life?

"Surrender to what
is. Let go of what
was. Have faith in
what will be."

Sonia Ricotti

JOURNALING PROMPT 9

What are some things that I am proud of in my life? How am I celebrating my successes and accomplishments? How can I celebrate myself more?

BELIEVE YOU CAN,
AND YOU'RE HALFWAY
THERE.

THEODORE ROOSEVELT

JOURNALING PROMPT 10

What is something that I have been avoiding or procrastinating on? Why have I been avoiding it? What steps can I take to overcome this resistance?

"Before you speak,
let your words
pass through three
gates: Is it true?
Is it necessary?
Is it kind?"

JOURNALING PROMPT 11

Do a little check in with yourself. What are the top three emotions that you've been feeling lately? Where do you feel them in your body? Describe them. What triggered those emotions?

BE KIND TO YOURSELF

Raise your words, not voice. It is rain that grows flowers, not thunder.

RUMI

JOURNALING PROMPT 12

Pay attention to the quality of your inner voice. What do you notice?

What are three self-defeating thoughts that show up in your self-talk? How can you reframe them to encourage yourself instead? How can you practice self-compassion and kindness towards yourself?

"In the midst of movement and chaos, keep stillness inside of you. No matter what is happening around you, you always have the power to tap into a place of calm and stillness within. By cultivating inner peace, you can navigate even the most turbulent of times with grace and ease. Remember, true strength comes from a place of inner serenity."

DEEPAK CHOPRA

JOURNALING PROMPT 13

Take a few minutes to focus on
your body. Just allow yourself to be
a mere observer and write down
any physical sensations you are
experiencing (such as tightness in
your shoulders or a feeling of
relaxation in your chest). Notice
how this loving awareness feels for
your body.

"Everything we hear is an opinion, not a fact. Everything we see is a perspective, not the truth. You have power over your mind – not outside events. Realize this, and you will find strength."

Marcus Aurelius

JOURNALING PROMPT 14

Take 5-10 minutes to focus on your breath. As you breathe in, focus on the sensation of the air entering your body. As you breathe out, focus on the sensation of the air leaving your body. Write down what you noticed and reflect what came up for you as you were practising this.

The mind is like water. When it's turbulent, it's difficult to see. When it's calm, everything becomes clear.

PRASAD MAHES

JOURNALING PROMPT 15

Take a few moments to mindfully observe your surroundings. Write down 3 things that you notice in detail. Focus on their essence, texture, color, shape or any other detail you observe. Practice being truly present with these objects of your attention.

We may not be responsible for the world that created our minds. but we can take responsibility for the mind with which we create our world.

GABOR MATÉ